HOUSTON PUBLIC LIBRARY

Friends of the
Houston Public Library

PowerKids Readers:
The Bilingual Library of the United States of America™

*Bilingual Edition
English/Spanish
Edición bilingüe*

WASHINGTON

JENNIFER WAY

TRADUCCIÓN AL ESPAÑOL: MARÍA CRISTINA BRUSCA

The Rosen Publishing Group's
PowerKids Press™ & **Editorial Buenas Letras**™
New York

Published in 2006 by The Rosen Publishing Group, Inc.
29 East 21st Street, New York, NY 10010

Copyright © 2006 by The Rosen Publishing Group, Inc.

All rights reserved. No part of this book may be reproduced in any form without permission in writing from the publisher, except by a reviewer.

First Edition

Photo Credits: Cover, p 31 (Volcano) © Craig Tuttle/Corbis; p. 5 © Joe Sohm/The Image Works; p. 7 © 2002 Geoatlas; pp. 9, 30 (The Evergreen State) © Terry W. Eggers/Corbis; p. 11 © Seattle Post-Intelligencer Collection; Museum of History and Industry/Corbis; p. 13 © Bettmann/Corbis; p. 15 © Corbis; pp. 17, 26 © Bill Ross/Corbis; p. 19 © Gary Holscher/Corbis; p. 21 © Chase Jarvis/Corbis; p. 23 © Nick Gunderson/Corbis; pp. 25, 30 (Capital) © Andre Jenny/The Image Works; p. 30 (Pink Rhododendron) © Pat O'Hara/Corbis; p. 30 (Willow Goldfinch) © Gary W. Carter/Corbis; p. 30 (Western Hemlock) © William Manning/Corbis; p. 31 (Crosby) © CinemaPhoto/Corbis; p. 31 (McCarthy) © Julio Donoso/Corbis Sygma; p. 31 (Cunningham, Gates) © Lynn Goldsmith/Corbis; p. 31 (Channing) © Roger Ressemeyer/Corbis; p. 31 (Hendrix) © Reuters/Corbis; p. 31 (Fur) © Connie Ricca/Corbis; p. 31 (Hiking) © Don Mason/Corbis.

Library of Congress Cataloging-in-Publication Data

Way, Jennifer.
  Washington / Jennifer Way ; traducción al español, María Cristina Brusca.- 1st ed.
     p. cm. - (The bilingual library of the United States of America)
  Includes bibliographical references and index.
  ISBN 1-4042-3113-7 (library binding)
  1. Washington (State)-Juvenile literature. I. Title. II. Series.
  F891.3.W39 2006
  979.7-dc22
                                          2005032641

Manufactured in the United States of America

Due to the changing nature of Internet links, Editorial Buenas Letras has developed an online list of Web sites related to the subject of this book. This site is updated regularly. Please use this link to access the list:

http://www.buenasletraslinks.com/ls/washington

Contents

1 Welcome to Washington 4
2 Washington Geography 6
3 Washington History 10
4 Living in Washington 18
5 Let´s Draw the Space Needle 26
   Timeline/ Washington Events 28–29
   Washington Facts 30
   Famous Washingtonians /Words to Know 31
   Resources/Word Count/Index 32

Contenido

1 Bienvenidos a Washington 4
2 Geografía de Washington 6
3 Historia de Washington 10
4 La vida en Washington 18
5 Dibujemos el edificio Space Needle 26
   Cronología/ Eventos en Washington 28–29
   Datos sobre Washington 30
   Washingtonianos famosos/ Palabras que debes saber 31
   Recursos/ Número de palabras/ Índice 32

Welcome to Washington

Washington is named for the United States' first president, George Washington. It is known as the Evergreen State. Evergreens are trees that stay green year-round.

Bienvenidos a Washington

Washington debe su nombre a George Washington, primer presidente de los Estados Unidos. Washington es conocido como el estado Siempre-Verde. Los árboles llamados siempre-verde conservan su color durante todo el año.

Washington Flag and State Seal

Bandera y escudo del estado de Washington

Washington Geography

Washington is in the Pacific Northwest. It borders the states of Idaho and Oregon and the country of Canada. Washington also borders the Pacific Ocean.

Geografía de Washington

Washington se encuentra en la región noroeste del país. Linda con los estados de Idaho y Oregón y con un país, Canadá. También linda con el océano Pacífico.

Map Key
Claves del mapa

- ● Major City / Ciudad principal
- ★ Capital / Capital
- ～ River / Río

CANADA / CANADÁ

Pacific Ocean / Océano Pacífico

- ● Bellingham
- ● Everett
- ● Seattle
- ● Tacoma
- ☆ Olympia
- ● Spokane
- ● Yakima

WASHINGTON

Columbia River / Río Columbia

OREGON / OREGÓN

IDAHO

Map of Washington
Mapa de Washington

Mount Rainier is one of the most famous mountains in Washington. It is part of the Cascade Mountains. Mount Rainier is a volcano.

El monte Rainier es uno de los más famosos de Washington. Es parte de la cadena de montañas Cascade. El monte Rainier es un volcán.

Mount Rainier

El monte Rainier

Washington History

The first people to live in Washington were Native Americans. One of the largest groups was the Chinook. The Chinook traded fish and furs with the Europeans who came to Washington.

Historia de Washington

Los primeros pobladores de Washington fueron nativos americanos. El grupo Chinook fue uno de los más grandes. Los Chinook intercambiaban pieles y pescado con los europeos que llegaron a Washington.

Chinook Woman and Her Child

Mujer Chinook con su hijo

Meriwether Lewis and William Clark traveled across the country. They were exploring land that the United States had bought from France. In 1805, they visited Washington. They made maps of the land there.

Meriwether Lewis y William Clark viajaron a través del país, explorando las tierras que los Estados Unidos le habían comprado a Francia. En 1805, viajaron por Washington y trazaron mapas de la región.

Meriwether Lewis and William Clark

Meriwether Lewis y William Clark

In 1883, the Northern Pacific Railroad finished its tracks in Tacoma, Washington. The railroad made it easier to travel and helped Tacoma grow. In seven years the city grew from 5,000 people to more than 30,000!

En 1883, las vías del ferrocarril Northern Pacific, llegaron hasta Tacoma, Washington, facilitando así los viajes al oeste. El ferrocarril hizo posible que Tacoma creciera. ¡En sólo siete años, la ciudad que tenía 5,000 habitantes, llegó a tener más de 30,000!

The Northern Pacific Railroad

Ferrocarril Northern Pacific

The Space Needle is Seattle's most famous landmark. It was built for the 1962 World's Fair. The Space Needle is 605 feet (184 m) tall. It has a deck near the top where you can have a view of the whole city.

El edificio Space Needle es el símbolo más famoso de Seattle. Fue construído para la Exposición Mundial de 1962. Tiene 605 pies (184 m) de altura. Desde su mirador, que está arriba, puedes ver toda la ciudad.

The Space Needle in Seattle, Washington

Edificio Space Needle, Washington

Living in Washington

Washington grows many crops. Washington is known for its cherries, asparagus, blackberries, apples, and grapes. Washington's Pacific coast also supplies a lot of the nation's fish.

La vida en Washington

En Washington hay muchos cultivos. El estado es conocido por sus cerezas, espárragos, zarzamoras, manzanas y uvas. Washington también provee a todo el país de pescado del océano Pacífico.

Apples from the Yakima Valley in Washington

Manzanas del valle Yakima, Washington

Many Washingtonians enjoy hiking on the trails that are found throughout the state. People also enjoy fishing and boating on the ocean or on Washington's rivers.

Muchos washingtonianos disfrutan de caminatas por los muchos senderos que se encuentran por todo el estado. La gente también pesca y navega en el océano y los ríos de Washington.

Fishing in the Methow River

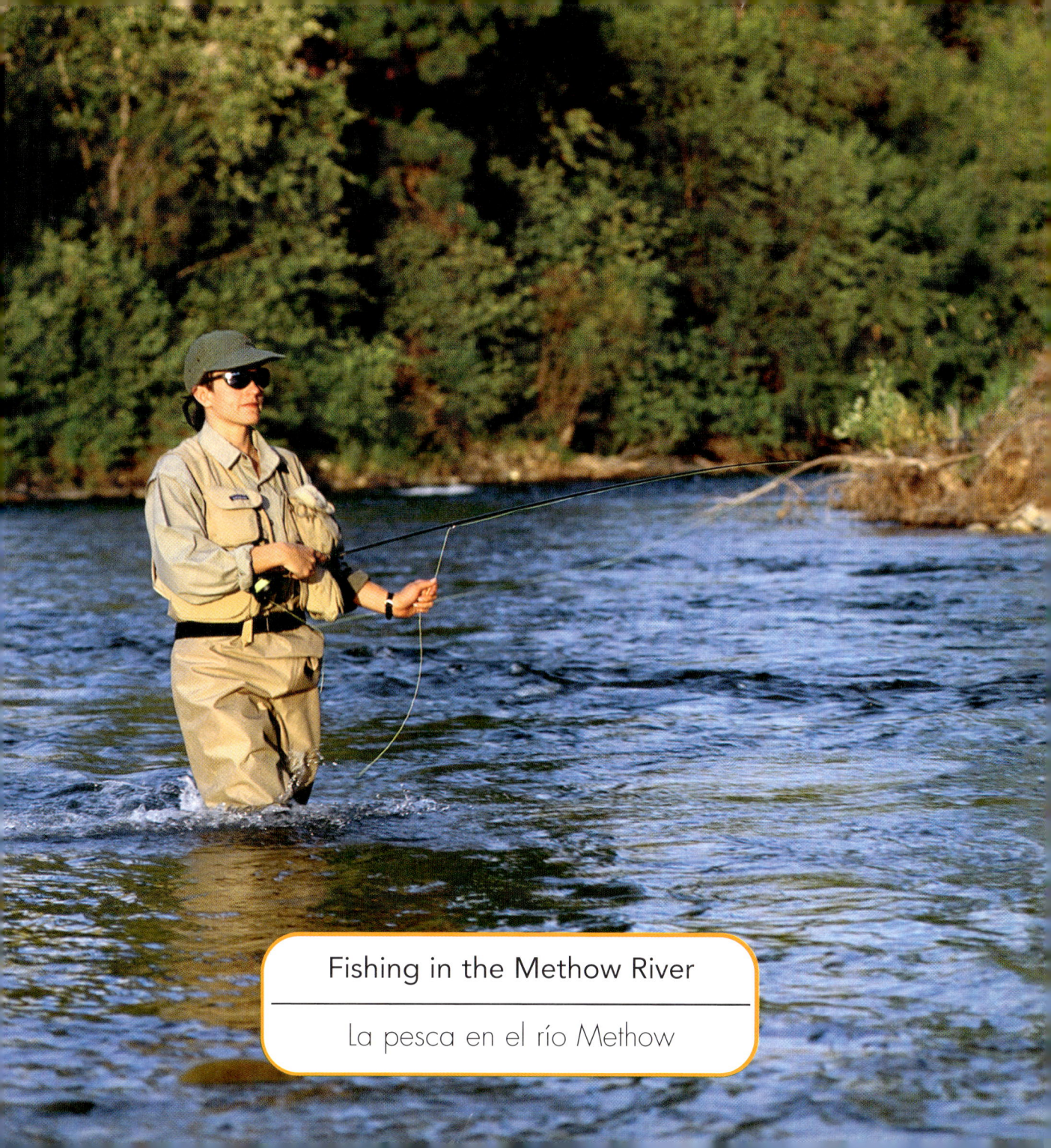

La pesca en el río Methow

The Children's Museum in Seattle is a great place to visit. It is a place where you can learn about nature and science. There is even a manmade mountain you can climb!

El Museo de los Niños de Seattle es un gran lugar para visitar. Allí puedes aprender temas científicos y de la naturaleza. ¡Hasta hay una montaña artificial que puedes escalar!

The Seattle Children's Museum

Museo de los Niños de Seattle

Seattle, Spokane, Tacoma, and Vancouver are the biggest cities in Washington. Olympia is the capital of the state.

Seattle, Spokane, Tacoma y Vancouver son las ciudades más grandes de Washington. Olympia es la capital del estado.

State Capitol Building in Olympia

Capitolio del estado en Olympia

Activity:
Let's Draw the Space Needle

Actividad:
Dibujemos el edificio Space Needle

1

Start by drawing slanted lines that cross, like the ones you see here.

Comienza por dibujar líneas inclinadas que se cruzan, como ves aquí.

2

Add two rectangles at the top.

Agrega dos rectángulos arriba.

3

Add two slanted rectangles to form a disc shape. Add another rectangle on top.

Agrega dos rectángulos sesgados arriba, para obtener una forma de disco. Agrega otro rectángulo encima de éstos.

4

Draw the top using a triangle and a square. Add the peak using a thin line.

Dibuja la parte superior trazando un triángulo y un cuadrado. Luego, agrega la aguja trazando una línea delgada.

5

Erase extra lines. Add shading and detail like the small windows.

Borra las líneas sobrantes y agrega sombras y detalles como, por ejemplo, las ventanas pequeñas.

Timeline / Cronología

British explorer James Cook maps Washington's coast.	**1778**	El explorador británico, James Cook, traza el mapa de la costa de Washington.
Spain builds the first European settlement in Washington.	**1792**	España establece la primera población europea en Washington.
Meriwether Lewis and William Clark explore Washington.	**1805**	Meriwether Lewis y William Clark exploran Washington.
Washington Territory is made.	**1853**	Se funda el Territorio de Washington.
Railroads link Washington to the East.	**1883**	El ferrocarril une Washington con los estados del este.
Washington becomes the forty-second state.	**1889**	Washington es admitido como el estado cuarenta y dos.
The Seattle Space Needle is finished.	**1961**	Se completa la construcción del edificio Space Needle.
Dixie Lee Ray becomes Washington's first woman governor.	**1976**	Dixie Lee Ray llega a ser la primera gobernadora de Washington.

Washington Events   Eventos en Washington

February | Febrero
Chili, Chowder and Dessert Cook Off and Bonfire in Elk | Fogata y cocina al aire libre: chile, *chowder* y postres, en Elk

May | Mayo
Menzies Discovery Days in Port Townsend | Días del descubrimiento de Menzies, en Port Townsend
Cinco de Mayo Fiesta in Pasco | Fiesta del Cinco de Mayo, en Pasco

June | Junio
Fall City Days in Fall City | Días de Fall City, en Fall City
Scottish Highland Games in Spokane | Juegos de las tierras altas escocesas, en Spokane

August | Agosto
Evergreen State Fair in Monroe | Feria del Estado Siempre-Verde, en Monroe
Walla Walla Fair and Frontier Days in Walla Walla | Feria de Walla Walla y Días de la frontera, en Walla Walla

September | Septiembre
Blackberry Festival in Bremerton | Festival de la zarzamora, en Bremerton
Salmon Festival in Leavenworth | Festival del salmón, en Leavenworth
Fiesta Viva! in Bothell | ¡Fiesta viva!, en Bothell
Italian Festival in Seattle | Festival italiano, en Seattle

November | Noviembre
Hmong New Year Celebration in Seattle | Celebración del año nuevo Hmong, en Seattle

Washington Facts/Datos sobre Washington

<u>Population</u> 6.1 million		<u>Población</u> 6.1 millones
<u>Capital</u> Olympia		<u>Capital</u> Olympia
<u>State Motto</u> *Alki* ("By and By")		<u>Lema del estado</u> *Alki* (esperanza en el futuro)
<u>State Flower</u> Pink Rhododendron		<u>Flor del estado</u> Rododendro rosado
<u>State Bird</u> Willow Goldfinch		<u>Ave del estado</u> Jilguero americano
<u>State Nickname</u> The Evergreen State		<u>Mote del estado</u> El Estado Siempre-Verde
<u>State Tree</u> Western Hemlock		<u>Árbol del estado</u> Cicuta occidental
<u>State Song</u> "Washington, My Home"		<u>Canción del estado</u> "Washington es mi hogar"

Famous Washingtonians/Washingtonianos famosos

Bing Crosby
(1903–1977)
Singer and actor
Cantante y actor

Mary McCarthy
(1912–1989)
Author
Escritora

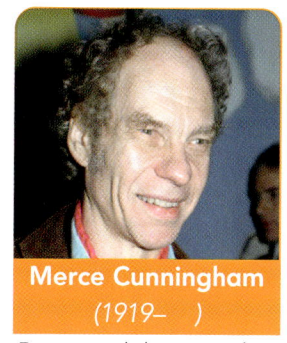

Merce Cunningham
(1919–   )
Dancer and choreographer
Bailarín y coreógrafo

Carol Channing
(1921–   )
Actress
Actriz

Jimi Hendrix
(1942–1970)
Musician
Músico

Bill Gates
(1955–   )
Founder of Microsoft
Fundador de Microsoft

Words to Know/Palabras que debes saber

border
frontera

fur
piel

hiking
caminar al aire libre

volcano
volcán

Here are more books to read about Washington:
Otros libros que puedes leer sobre Washington:

In English/En inglés:

E Is for Evergreen: A Washington Alphabet
by Marie Smith
Sleeping Bear Press, 2004

Washington
by Stephen Feinstein
Enslow Publishers, 2003

Words in English: 318

Palabras en español: 333

Index

B
borders, 6

C
Cascade Mountains, 8
Children's Museum, 22
Chinook, 10
Clark, William, 12
crops, 18

E
Evergreen State, 4

L
Lewis, Meriwether, 12

M
Mount Rainier, 8

N
Northern Pacific Railroad, 14

P
Pacific Northwest, 6

W
Washington, George, 4

Índice

C
Cascade, montañas, 8
Chinook, 10
Clark, William, 12
cultivos, 18

E
Estado Siempre-Verde, 4

F
ferrocarril Northern Pacific, 14
fronteras, 6

L
Lewis, Meriwether, 12

M
Monte Rainier, 8
Museo de los Niños, 22

W
Washington, George, 4

+ SP   **Friends of the**
979.7 W   **Houston Public Library**

Way, Jennifer.
Washington
Stanaker JUV CIRC
07/06